Mother Gertie

A Mother Goose

Terrie Sizemore

Mother Gertie : A Mother Goose

Printed in the United States of America

A 2 Z Press LLC

3670 Woodbridge Rd

Deland, FL 32720

bestlittleonlinebookstore.com

sizemore3630@aol.com

440-241-3126

ISBN: 978-1-954191-89-1

Dedication

To all moms everywhere

This Book Belongs To:

_____

Goose Gertie wanted to be a mom too.
Watching over her very own chicks
is all she wanted to do.

Gertie waited and waited hoping
for some goslings.
She knew they would be
the cutest little things!

Gertie made a nest and sat
on big goose eggs for days.
In hopes to hatch little ones
to love in motherly ways.

But Gertie babies did not come.
Even though she did so want some.

Then, one sunny morning,
with a soft little quack,
Came a yellow and black
duckling – the first of the pack.

Then along came four beautiful others,
And, suddenly, the ducklings
had three mothers!

Those five little ducklings
took to Gertie Goose,
They followed her everywhere – there
were five ducklings on the loose !

With playful delight, they
all went everywhere,
Through tall, wild grass –
always in Gertie's care.

All the babies rely on Gertie's protection.
For geese are skilled at danger detection !

Gertie stays close by and
watches the ducklings each day,
She makes sure they are
safe in every way.

Gertie leads the entire duckling parade.
What a great mommy Gertie has made!

Gertie's so happy, now it's easy to see,
It's because she has
five little duckling babies !

The ducklings love Gertie like
she's their own mother.
They all know they
belong to each other.

Under Gertie's wing, daily,
they learnt something new.
And with every soft quack,
their bond grew and grew.

Gertie and the ducks are
a blended family and full of cheer,
In their loving world,
they all hold each other dear.

HOW
MAKING
FAMILY
by Gertie Goose

For family comes in many different ways,
Goose Gertie has found great joy in her days.
She longed for babies and has them now,
She really doesn't mind how !

HAPPY FAMILY DAY!

Gertie says it doesn't matter
who you are or what you do,
As long as you have love in your
heart, you can be a mom too !

The End

Mother Gertie is based on a real goose I own. She did sit on eggs that did not hatch, but shared the ducklings with Olivia and Emily

Gertie and the Ducklings

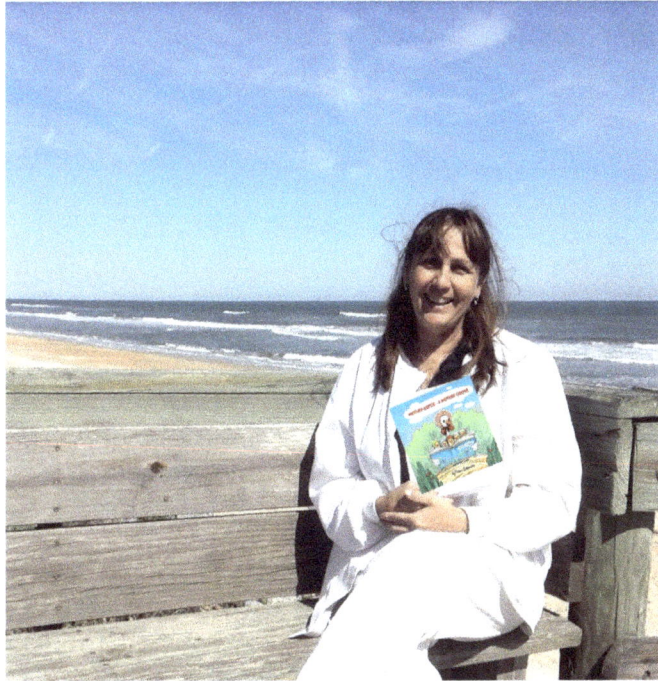

Terrie Sizemore has cherished
children's literature for
many years. She has taught
children most of her life
and feels reading and art are fun and
exciting and invaluable parts
of every child's life.
She hopes every little reader enjoys
this book as much as she
enjoyed creating it.

A2Z Press LLC

A2Z Press LLC
published this work.
A2Z Press LLC is a
publishing company
created by Terrie Sizemore
for the purpose
of publishing literary works by new
and aspiring writers. All content is
G-rated. We welcome your submissions
of ideas for children's literature as well
as adult and self-help topics.
Science and medicine, holidays and
other interesting topics are all welcome.
Submit queries to sizemore3630@aol.com or
3670 Woodbridge Rd
Deland, FL 32720

Visit our Website

Visit terriesizemorestoryteller.com or bestlittleonlinebookstore.com for our latest titles and gifts for everyone.

Other Books by
A 2 Z Press Authors

TV Mouse

There is a Poem Inside of Me

Never 'TOO' Wonderful

Butterfly Beauties and Magical Moths

Little Leaf Louise

The Day the Cat Said 'MOO!'

Fabulous Frogs and Terrific Toads

Golden Tales: Havoc in Rome

Crabs are Incredible

Fairy Hairy Trouble!

And MORE!

www.ingramcontent.com/pod-product-compliance
Lightning Source LLC
Chambersburg PA
CBHW042333030426
42335CB00027B/3327